P9-CQK-689

# THE UNSTOPPABLE GARRETT MORGAN

## INVENTOR, ENTREPRENEUR, HERO

BY **JOAN DICICCO**

ILLUSTRATED BY **EBONY GLENN**

Lee & Low Books Inc.

*New York*

ACKNOWLEDGEMENTS

My deepest thanks to my editor, Kandace Coston, for championing this story with a passion that matched my own; her inspired vision, dedication to historical accuracy, and expert guidance throughout; and to the entire editorial team at Lee & Low for saying "Yes!" to my dream of putting Garrett Morgan's story into the hands of children.

A sincere thank you to Margaret Bernstein, award-winning journalist and Director of Advocacy & Community Initiatives at WKYC, Cleveland, through whom I discovered the thread that wove the narrative of Garrett's story, for generously lending her time, knowledge, and support.

To local historian and Hopewell Museum volunteer Sharon B. Fields, my heartfelt thanks for providing valuable insight into Garrett Morgan's early life in Kentucky.

Many thanks to Ann Sindelar, Library Research Center Reference Supervisor at Western Reserve Historical Society, for facilitating my access to the Garrett Morgan Papers and for her unwavering patience while answering my countless questions.

And infinite gratitude to my critique group community for their insights, wisdom, honesty, and enthusiasm. Thank you for keeping me grounded while lifting me up.—J.D.

Text copyright © 2019 by Joan DiCicco
Illustrations copyright © 2019 by Ebony Glenn
All rights reserved. No part of this book may be reproduced, transmitted, or stored
in an information retrieval system in any form or by any means, electronic, mechanical,
photocopying, recording, or otherwise, without written permission from the publisher.

LEE & LOW BOOKS Inc., 95 Madison Avenue, New York, NY 10016
leeandlow.com
Manufactured in China by Toppan
Edited by Kandace Coston
Designed by Christy Hale
Production by The Kids at Our House
The text is set in Octavian
The illustrations are rendered digitally

10   9   8   7   6   5   4   3   2   1
First Edition

Library of Congress Cataloging-in-Publication Data
Names: DiCicco, Joan, author. | Glenn, Ebony, illustrator.
Title: The unstoppable Garrett Morgan : inventor, entrepreneur, hero / by
Joan DiCicco ; illustrated by Ebony Glenn.
Description: First edition. | New York : Lee & Low Books Inc. [2019] |
Includes bibliographical references. | Audience: Ages 7-11. | Audience:
Grades 4 to 6.
Identifiers: LCCN 2018060117 | ISBN 9781620145647 (hardcover : alk. paper)
Subjects: LCSH: Morgan, Garrett A., 1877-1963—Juvenile literature. | African
American inventors—Biography—Juvenile literature. | Inventors—United
States—Biography—Juvenile literature.
Classification: LCC TJ140.M67 D53 2019 | DDC 609.2 [B]—dc23
LC record available at https://lccn.loc.gov/2018060117

*To my husband, and in memory of my father—*

*for inspiring the best in me —J.D.*

*Clang! Clang! Clang!* Young Garrett Morgan
awoke to the sound of a ringing brass bell. He ran
to the window and saw plumes of black smoke rising
from the neighboring farm. He woke his younger brother Frank,
grabbed the water buckets, and raced to help.

These types of fires were common for sharecroppers like Garrett's parents.
Their shacks were made of wood and tar paper that burned smoky, hot, and fast.
If people were trapped inside, rescuers had nothing to protect themselves from
poisonous smoke.

By the time Garrett and Frank arrived, only a burned-out shell of the house
remained. As they walked back home, the gears in Garrett's clever mind turned,
trying to think of a way to help.

The son of freed slaves, Garrett was born in Claysville, Kentucky, in 1877, the seventh of eleven children. As sharecroppers, the Morgans worked on land owned by a different family in exchange for a share of the crop at harvest time. After the cost of their housing, farm tools, and seed was subtracted from their share, they often found themselves in debt. Innovation became a way of life for Garrett. If his family needed something they didn't have, he figured out a way to make it himself.

By the age of fourteen, curious and creative Garrett was restless for a better life. Segregation was strictly enforced in the South, leaving few prospects for African Americans. Garrett went north to find greater opportunity.

Garrett arrived in Cincinnati, Ohio, with pennies in his pocket. Having just a sixth-grade education and few skills, he took the only job he was offered—as a handyman for a wealthy landowner.

Although he worked long days, Garrett never tired of learning. Each week he set aside money for a private tutor and continued his studies.

Four years later, Garrett moved further north, hoping to find a better job. Cleveland was becoming a major manufacturing center for the clothing industry. Throughout the garment district, workers used machines to make things that had once been crafted by hand. It was here, with modern machinery whizzing and whirling, ticking and clicking, that Garrett's creative nature soared.

    While working as a janitor for a clothing manufacturer, Garrett noticed that
the drive belts on the sewing machines became slack after a while and often broke.
Broken machines frustrated the workers, whose pay depended upon the number of
garments they produced.

    As he'd learned to do on the farm, Garrett solved the problem through his own
innovation. He invented a simple but effective belt tightener that adjusted the
slack and helped the machine run longer, smoother, and faster. Garrett's boss was
so impressed by his creativity that he promoted Garrett to work as a repairman.

It wasn't long before word got around that Garrett could fix just about anything. A competing manufacturer offered him a job, and in 1906, Garrett became the company's first black machinist.

There, Garrett met a German seamstress named Mary Hasek. Mary was equally bright, creative, and hard-working. Garrett and Mary were instantly drawn to each other. But black men were not permitted to talk to white female employees. Even a simple conversation with Mary brought a stern warning from Garrett's supervisor. But Garrett didn't give up. By now, he had overcome so many obstacles that he lived by a motto:

*"If a man puts something to block your way,*

*the first time you go **around** it,*

*the second time you go **over** it,*

*and the third time you go **through** it."*

This way of thinking made Garrett unstoppable!

To be with Mary, Garrett figured out a way to go *around* the obstacle. He quit his job and opened a sewing machine repair shop. Mary admired Garrett's boldness. In 1908, Mary and Garrett were married.

With Mary's skill as an expert seamstress, Garrett expanded the business and began manufacturing affordable clothing for Cleveland's growing black middle class. They named their business *Morgan's Cut Rate Ladies Clothing*. By 1909, they had thirty-two employees working on machinery built by Garrett himself.

Ding! Ding! Ding! A fire engine's bell rang out as a team of horses whizzed by. Their manes whipped in the wind like the flames racing through the building at the end of the block. The firefighters prepared to go in—holding their leather helmets in front of their faces to block the heat and smoke. Their efforts proved useless as they stumbled out, gasping for air.

When Garrett heard about the tragedy, memories of the fires he had witnessed as a boy sparked to life. Though many years had passed, he realized that even big-city firefighters lacked the equipment they needed to save victims. With the gears of his creative mind already turning, Garrett headed to his workshop, determined to find a way to help firefighters breathe in smoke-filled spaces.

Garrett knew that smoke and deadly fumes rose with the heat of a fire, leaving a layer of fresh air near the ground. He needed to create a device that could capture this fresh air and lift it up for firefighters to breathe.

He fashioned a heat-resistant canvas helmet with two long tubes attached: one for inhaling, lined with a wet sponge to cool and filter the air; and one for exhaling, with a valve to keep the stale air from getting back in. The tubes joined halfway down the wearer's back to become one tube dangling close to the ground in the layer of breathable air.

Garrett spent three years crafting and refining his invention. His brother Frank helped him test the different helmets. After countless long nights falling asleep at his workbench, Garrett finally succeeded. He called his new invention the Safety Hood.

In 1912, Garrett applied for a patent, which gives an inventor the sole right to make, use, and sell an invention. When his patent was granted, Garrett entered the Safety Hood in the 1914 International Exposition of Safety and Sanitation in New York City. Wearing his device for protection, Garrett entered a tent filled with smoldering sulfur, ammonia, and tar, remaining there for more than twenty minutes. To the shock and amazement of the crowd, he emerged unharmed. The Safety Hood won the Grand Prize Gold Medal.

Garrett traveled across the country, demonstrating the Safety Hood to fire departments. Many were impressed by the brilliant invention but refused to consider the Safety Hood when they discovered Garrett was African American. Determined not to let prejudice stop him, Garrett called upon his motto and went *over* the obstacle this time. He asked a white friend to pretend to be him while Garrett posed as his assistant modeling the hood. Some fire chiefs put the invention through their own rigorous tests, but the Safety Hood exceeded their expectations. Orders for Garrett's device flooded in!

On July 25, 1916, Garrett Morgan and his Safety Hood would face the greatest test of all.

*Rrrring! Rrrring! Rrrring!* Garrett's telephone rang out in the middle of the night. An explosion had ripped through a tunnel at the Cleveland Waterworks, trapping workers in smoke and deadly fumes hundreds of feet below Lake Erie. One of the rescuers had seen Garrett's demonstration. Only the Safety Hood could save the men underground.

With no time to waste, Garrett called Frank and raced to help.

When Garrett arrived at the Waterworks, he handed out protective hoods to the firefighters, police, and other volunteers. But the men refused to join him.

"Two other rescue parties went down and have failed to return," Mayor Davis said.

Garrett knew time was running out. "I'll take a chance," he said.

Frank stepped forward. "I'll go with you."

A man named Tom Clancy spoke up. "My father is in there. I will go." Another man volunteered as well.

True to his motto, Garrett Morgan went straight *through* the obstacle!

As they descended into the tunnel, the faint light of dawn gave way to absolute darkness. While the rest of the men waited near the elevator, Garrett donned the Safety Hood and felt his way toward the iron door that led to the tunnel.

Garrett had never tested his invention underground. He didn't know if the Safety Hood could withstand the compressed air pressure within the tunnel. He didn't know if it would keep him alive. There was only one way to find out. He turned the latch, opened the door, and stepped through.

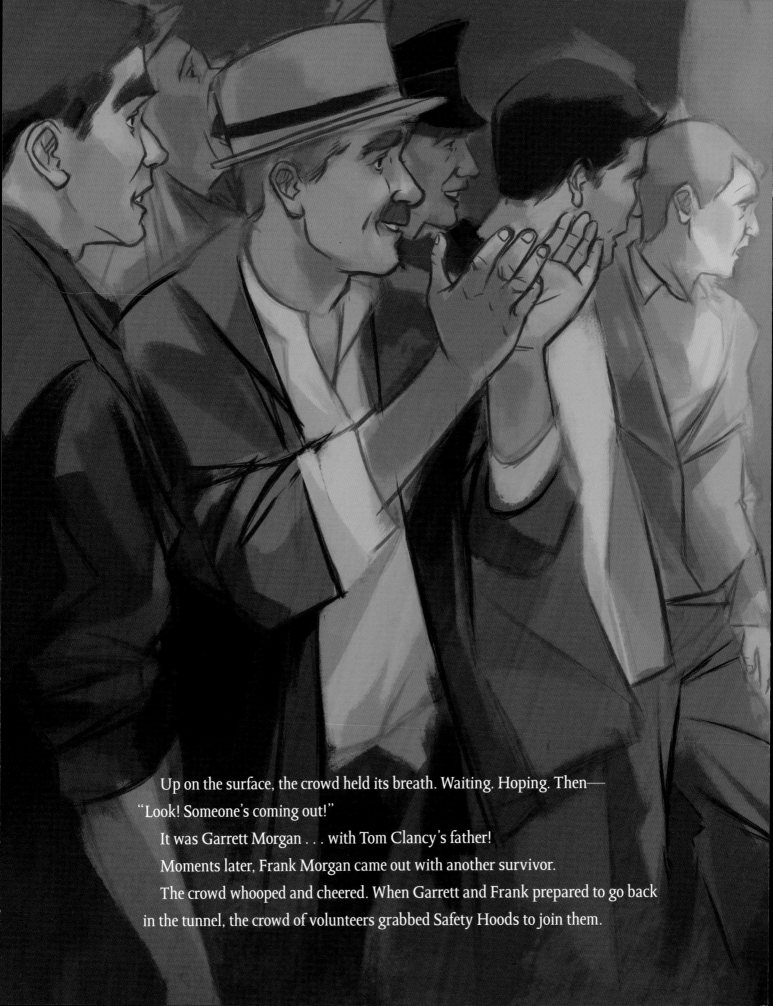

Up on the surface, the crowd held its breath. Waiting. Hoping. Then—

"Look! Someone's coming out!"

It was Garrett Morgan . . . with Tom Clancy's father!

Moments later, Frank Morgan came out with another survivor.

The crowd whooped and cheered. When Garrett and Frank prepared to go back
in the tunnel, the crowd of volunteers grabbed Safety Hoods to join them.

The next day, the story of the rescued men was front-page news. But Garrett and his brother were not given credit for their bravery. Only the white volunteers were named and later awarded the Carnegie Medal for Heroism.

Many people had heard of Garrett's heroic actions and grew angry that he was excluded. Dozens of businessmen and elected officials wrote letters to the Carnegie Foundation, asking them to correct the injustice. When these efforts didn't work, the Citizen's Committee, a self-appointed group of community leaders, came together to acknowledge Garrett's achievements and service to Cleveland. They held a ceremony and presented him with a solid gold, diamond-studded medal inscribed *To Garrett A. Morgan, Our Most Honored and Bravest Citizen.*

Garrett Morgan's desire to help people was a lifelong pursuit. If he saw a need for something, he used his ingenuity and resources to fill it. He continued to improve the Safety Hood, and in 1917, as the United States prepared to enter World War I, the Safety Hood was developed into the gas mask that saved thousands of American soldiers' lives.

When Garrett and other black businessmen were barred from advertising in white-owned newspapers, he started *Call*, a newspaper in which African Americans could promote their businesses and read fair-minded news about the black community, written by black reporters.

After Garrett witnessed a terrible collision between a horse-drawn carriage and a motor car at an intersection, he invented a more effective traffic signal. In addition to telling drivers when to GO and STOP, his patented device also included a STOP ALL position that stopped traffic in all directions, allowing cars and pedestrians traveling in one direction to clear the street before traffic traveling in the opposite direction began.

With determination and courage, Garrett Morgan went *around*, *over*, and *through* every obstacle between him and his goal to help others. Today his legacy is all around us. Whenever firefighters rescue people from smoke-filled buildings or motorists and pedestrians safely cross an intersection, we have a brave inventor to thank: the unstoppable Garrett Morgan.

1877 March 4: Born Garrett Augustus Morgan in Claysville, Kentucky, a segregated section of Paris, Kentucky, that was established after the Civil War to house freed slaves now working as sharecroppers.

1891 Leaves his family's farm to seek a better life across the Ohio River in Cincinnati.

1895 Moves to the city of Cleveland, Ohio—a major center of clothing manufacturing—where he finds a job sweeping floors at Root and McBride, a wholesaler of dry goods and notions. Later, he works for H. Black Company and L. N. Gross, both of which manufacture women's clothing.

1901 Develops and sells the rights to his first invention, a sewing machine belt tightener.

1905 Discovers that a polish used to keep sewing needles from scorching fabric also works as a hair straightener.

1906 Hired by Prince-Wolf Company, a manufacturer of women's suits and cloaks, as their first black machinist.

   Meets Mary Hasek, a white immigrant seamstress from Bavaria, Germany.

1907 Strikes out on his own, opening a sewing machine sales and repair shop in the heart of Cleveland's garment district.

1908 September 22: Marries Mary in Ohio, the first state to legalize interracial marriage.

   A fire rips through Kresge's Department Store, engulfing the five-story building block, and kills seven people. This event inspires Garrett to begin work on his Safety Hood.

   Becomes a founding member of the Cleveland Colored Men's Association, an organization that later merged with the National Association for the Advancement of Colored People (NAACP).

1909 Garrett and Mary combine their talents and open a tailoring shop where they hire thirty-two employees to manufacture women's clothing. With Mary's expertise, they develop a successful line of children's clothing. Garrett customizes the factory's machinery through inventions like the zigzag sewing attachment for manually operated machines.

1912 Garrett and Mary welcome the birth of their first son, John Pierpont, named after J. P. Morgan Jr., an American banker, philanthropist, and personal friend.

   Perfects his design for the Safety Hood and applies for a U.S. patent.

1913 Establishes the G. A. Morgan Hair Refining Company to sell a line of hair care products and market the discovery he has kept secret since 1905—the sewing needle polish that also straightens curly hair. Develops the industrial polish into a cream that's safe for human skin. The product is hugely successful.

Credited as being the first African American in Cleveland to own an automobile.

1914    A second son is born, Garrett Augustus Morgan Jr.

Awarded his patent for the Safety Hood. With several white businessmen from his community, Garrett establishes the National Safety Device Company to market it. He travels the country, demonstrating the Safety Hood to fire departments.

December: Wins the Grand Prize Gold Medal for this invention at the Second International Exposition of Sanitation and Safety in New York.

1916    February: Hosts an all-night gala to celebrate the opening of his new factory, which he built next to his home on Harlem Avenue. Here, he houses the G. A. Morgan Hair Refining Company, which now manufactures a full line of hair care products for African Americans. This venture makes him wealthy enough to devote all of his time to his inventions.

July 25: Uses the Safety Hood to help rescue and recover victims at the Cleveland Waterworks Tunnel disaster.

1917    The Carnegie Hero Commission refuses to acknowledge Garrett for their award. A group of local citizens honors his bravery with the presentation of a solid gold, diamond-studded medal.

Garrett is made an honorary member of the International Association of Fire Chiefs.

The Safety Hood is developed into the first gas mask and is used in World War I to protect soldiers from deadly mustard gas. The invention helps to save thousands of lives.

1919    Garrett and Mary's third son, Cosmo Henry Morgan, is born.

TOP: An image of Garrett Morgan's Safety Hood after further developments, circa 1920s. BOTTOM: Garrett Morgan and volunteers bringing the first victim out of the tunnel after the Cleveland Waterworks Disaster of 1916. Garrett Morgan is wearing the Safety Hood.

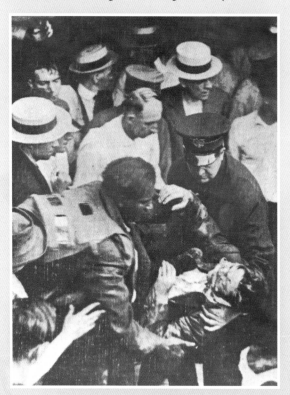

Garrett Morgan's traffic signal design.

1920    Establishes *Call*, a local newspaper for and about the African American community.

1922    Invents a traffic signal that includes an "all stop" command, making intersections safer for pedestrians and all forms of transportation.

1923    Receives a patent for his traffic signal, which he sells to the General Electric Company for a large sum of money. Uses this money to purchase a 121-acre farm on which he builds the Wakeman Country Club, the first all-black country club in Ohio.

1929    Loses most of his money in the October stock market crash that plunges the United States and the rest of the world into the Great Depression.

1931    Runs for a seat on the Cleveland City Council to address the needs of the black community. Although he does not win the election, he is praised by many for his efforts to improve housing conditions, create better-lit city streets, expand the city-owned hospital, and provide financial relief for thousands of unemployed people during the Great Depression.

1934    Garrett's brother Frank dies at the age of 52. Garrett asks the Cleveland City Council to pay for Frank's burial with the money Garrett had been fighting to receive as compensation for lingering health problems stemming from the

Waterworks Explosion. They agree.

1943    Develops glaucoma, an eye disease, and begins to lose his vision.

1953    The Pi Chapter of Alpha Phi Alpha, the first African American intercollegiate Greek-lettered fraternity, makes him an honorary member. Other members include jazz musician Duke Ellington, civil rights leader Rev. Dr. Martin Luther King Jr., and the first African American Supreme Court Justice, Thurgood Marshall.

1956    Awarded a patent for a de-curling comb.

1958    Garrett and Mary celebrate their 50th wedding anniversary.

1960    Despite now being completely blind due to glaucoma, invents an electric hair-curling comb.

1963    July 27: Dies at age 86 in Cleveland, Ohio, while preparing a retrospective of his work for the Centennial Celebration of Emancipation in Chicago, Illinois.

1974    His birthplace, Claysville, Kentucky, is renamed Garrett Morgan Place.

1991    The Cleveland Waterworks Plant is renamed the Garrett A. Morgan Water Treatment Plant in honor of his heroism.

1994    A memorial plaque is placed at his grave, paid for by money raised by Boulevard Elementary School students of Cleveland Heights, Ohio.

# BIBLIOGRAPHY

Alpha Phi Alpha Fraternity, Inc. "The Founding of Alpha Phi Alpha." Accessed March 1, 2019. https://apa1906.net/our-history/.

Bernstein, Margaret. "Inventor Garrett Morgan, Cleveland's Fierce Bootstrapper." Accessed July 21, 2015. http://teachingcleveland.org/inventor-garrett-morgan-clevelands-fierce-bootstrapper-by-margaret-bernstein/.

Case Western Reserve University. "Garment Industry." Accessed February 22, 2018. http://case.edu/ech/articles/g/garment-industry/.

————. "Morgan, Garrett A." Accessed June 6, 2015. http://case.edu/ech/articles/m/morgan-garrett-a/.

Cleveland Public Library Facebook post July 13, 2017. Accessed March 1, 2019. https://www.facebook.com/clevelandpubliclibrary/posts/tbt-a-fire-broke-out-at-kresge-co-dime-store-2025-ontario-st-when-the-fireworks-/10155510858099834/.

Garrett A. Morgan Papers. Western Reserve Historical Society Library, Cleveland, OH.

Garrett A. Morgan Scrapbook. Western Reserve Historical Society Library, Cleveland, OH.

The Encyclopedia of Cleveland History. "Root & McBride Co." Accessed September 6, 2016. http://case.edu/ech/articles/r/root-mcbride-co.

Fire Engineering. "The History of Firefighter Personal Protective Equipment." Accessed November 10, 2016. http://www.fireengineering.com/articles/2008/06/the-history-of-firefighter-personal-protective-equipment.

Morgan, Garrett A. Breathing device. U.S. Patent 1,113,675, filed August 19, 1912, and issued October 13, 1914.

Morgan, Garrett A. and J. J. Sullivan. Garrett Morgan's first-hand account of his actions during the rescue attempt following the July 24, 1916, Cleveland Waterworks Tunnel Disaster. Garrett A. Morgan Papers. Western Reserve Historical Society Library. Cleveland, Ohio.

Ohio History Connection. "Heroism Has No Color Line, Local Men Prove." Accessed February 21, 2017. http://dbs.ohiohistory.org/africanam/html/pagec3c8.html?ID=6140.

————. "Leading Citizens Plan to Honor G. A. Morgan, Tunnel Hero, on Sunday." Accessed February 21, 2017. http://dbs.ohiohistory.org/africanam/html/pageefl12.html?ID=6322.

Oluonye, Mary N. *Garrett Augustus Morgan: Businessman, Inventor, Good Citizen*. Bloomington, IN: AuthorHouse, 2008.

The Rhode Island College. "Garrett Augustus Morgan 1877-1963 Cleveland Businessman and Inventor." Accessed June 9, 2015. http://ric.edu/faculty/rpotter/morgan.html.

Teaching Cleveland. "Garrett A. Morgan, Gas Mask Inventor Dim Memory Here." Accessed June 6, 2015. http://teachingcleveland.org/wp-content/uploads/2010/06/garrett%20mnorgan%20story%20pd%2021675%2043d.pdf.

University of Kentucky. "Notable Kentucky African Americans—Claysville and Other Neighborhoods." Accessed September 6, 2016. http://nkaa.uky.edu/nkaa/items/show/316.

Watch the Yard. "Twenty Famous Alpha Phi Alpha Members You Should Know." Accessed March 1, 2019. https://www.watchtheyard.com/alphas/twenty-famous-alpha-phi-alpha-members-you-should-know/17/.

The Western Reserve Fire Museum and Education Center. "Northeast Ohio Fire History." Accessed March 1, 2019. https://wrfmc.com/northeast-ohio-fire-history/.